38106000016273

WHAT HAPPENS TO YOUR BODY

WHEN YOU RUN

| SIMONE PAYMENT |

rosen publishing's
rosen central

New York

Published in 2010 by The Rosen Publishing Group, Inc.
29 East 21st Street, New York, NY 10010

Library of Congress Cataloging-in-Publication Data

Payment, Simone.
What happens to your body when you run / Simone Payment.—1st ed.
    p. cm.—(The how and why of exercise)
Includes bibliographical references and index.
ISBN-13: 978-1-4358-5306-5 (library binding)
1. Running—Juvenile literature. 2. Physical fitness—Juvenile literature. 3. Exercise—Juvenile literature. I. Title.
GV1061.P38 2010
613.7'172—dc22

2008055150

Manufactured in Malaysia

CONTENTS

INTRODUCTION

Are you as healthy as you could be? Do you exercise regularly and eat right? If you do, you know that exercise and good nutrition can make you feel great. However, about one out of three children and young adults in America is over the ideal weight. Another one out of three is borderline overweight. If you fall into either category, now's the time to get active. Once you learn the benefits of regular exercise, it will be easy to see why being physically active is so important for your physical and mental health. Running might be the exercise that's right for you.

Regular exercise has many significant benefits. It can help you maintain proper body weight. It improves the health and strength of the heart and lungs. Exercise can lead to improvements in posture and coordination. Exercise also relieves stress, can improve mood, and can help you sleep better. Exercise might even make you smarter! A recent study by the California Department of Education showed that students who are in good physical condition score higher on standard achievement tests.

Running can be a good way to get regular exercise. For one thing, no one needs to teach you to run. It's something

Running isn't a seasonal sport—you can run any time of year, which makes this an ideal and practical form of exercise.

you've always done. Other than a good pair of shoes, you won't need any special equipment—such as a bike or weights or a racquet. You can run in many places and you don't need a special field or court as you might for other sports. And you can run in most weather conditions, which makes it an ideal exercise.

What Happens When You Run?

CHAPTER 1

The human body is an amazing machine. It is made up of many different systems. Each system performs a variety of functions. All the systems work together to keep you breathing, growing, talking—and running. The major systems in your body are the circulatory, digestive, endocrine, immune, musculoskeletal, nervous, and respiratory systems. All of these systems play a role in your ability to run. However, some play a larger role than others.

The Circulatory System

The circulatory system is made up of blood and the blood vessels that carry your blood around your body. Your heart is the other major part of the circulatory system. It pumps your blood, which carries oxygen to your whole body. Your blood also carries nutrients and other chemicals, such as hormones.

When your blood passes through your lungs, it picks up oxygen from the air you inhale. The oxygen-rich blood then moves away from your heart through blood vessels called arteries. The farther away from your lungs the blood gets, the less oxygen it carries. When the blood reaches areas farthest from your lungs, there is little oxygen left. The pumping of your heart keeps the blood moving, and the blood then returns to your lungs to pick up more oxygen. The blood comes back to the lungs through your veins.

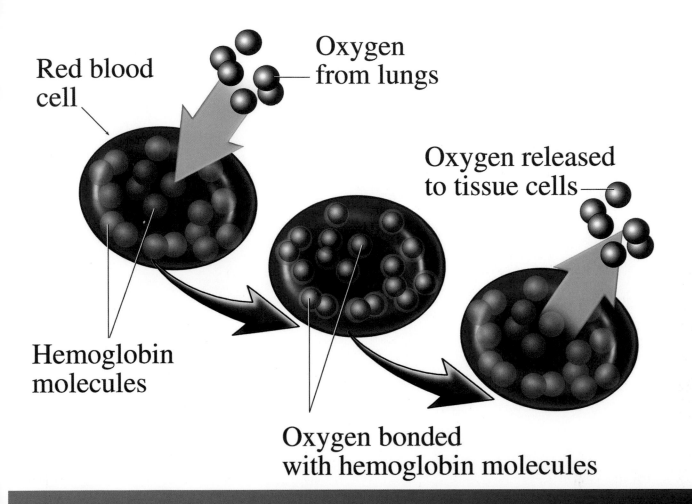

Red blood cell

Oxygen from lungs

Oxygen released to tissue cells

Hemoglobin molecules

Oxygen bonded with hemoglobin molecules

Red blood cells are the components of the blood that pick up oxygen from your lungs and transport it to other parts of your body.

The Digestive System

The digestive system processes the food you eat into nutrients that your body needs to grow, move, and keep you warm. Major parts of the digestive system include your mouth, esophagus, stomach, and small and large intestines. The liver, pancreas, and gallbladder also play a role in digestion. They make or store substances that help digest food.

There are more than 200 bones in the human body and as many as 840 muscles. They all work together to allow us to move.

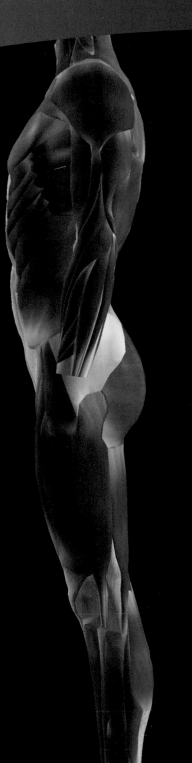

The Endocrine System

The system that controls production of hormones is called the endocrine system. Hormones are needed for growth, and they control your mood. Your brain and glands are parts of the endocrine system.

The Immune System

To fight germs, your body calls on the immune system. Lymph vessels are located throughout the body. They move fluid through the body, and at various places—called lymph nodes—germs are filtered out.

The Musculoskeletal System

Your body's musculoskeletal system is made up of two hundred bones in your skeleton and seven hundred muscles attached to your skeleton. Ligaments connect bones to other bones. Tendons attach muscles to bones. The musculoskeletal system gives your body shape and allows you to move.

There are three types of muscles in your body: skeletal, smooth, and cardiac. Skeletal muscles are attached to your bones. They help you move and connect the bones of your skeleton. Smooth muscles are found in parts of your body like your stomach or intestine. You don't consciously control these muscles as you can your skeletal muscles. Smooth muscle movements happen automatically. For example, your stomach moves your food using smooth muscles. The third type of muscle is cardiac. It is found only in your heart. Like smooth muscles, you don't consciously control your cardiac muscle.

The Nervous System

The nervous system is your body's control and communication system. It is made up of your brain, your spinal cord, and your nerves. Your brain controls your conscious thoughts. It also receives and sends messages to all parts of your body. It can regulate how fast your heart beats or "tell" your hand to move quickly away from a hot stove. The brain lets your body know it's time to eat by signaling hunger. It can also let your body know it's time to stop eating by signaling that you are full.

Exercise Physiology

The ancient Greeks were the first to study the effects of exercise on the body. This study is called exercise physiology. A Greek named Galen (131–201 CE) was a doctor who studied and wrote about the benefits of exercise. He also wrote about the importance of good nutrition. Galen performed experiments to study anatomy and learn how exercise changes the human body. His experiments allowed him to offer exercise advice, such as how long to exercise.

The Respiratory System

The respiratory system controls your breathing and allows the body to take in oxygen and exhale carbon dioxide. Your lungs and the airways from your lungs to your mouth and nose are the major parts of this system. Although it is part of the muscu-loskeletal system, your diaphragm is an important part of the respiratory system. It is a powerful muscle located below your lungs. It moves up and down to allow your lungs to expand and contract.

The Systems at Work When You Exercise

The three systems that play the biggest roles when you exercise are the circulatory, respiratory, and musculoskeletal systems. The rest of your body's systems play a role in exercise, too, but not as big a role.

When your body is resting, your heart pumps about seventy times per minute and it never stops. The pumping of your heart moves blood around the body, carrying oxygen to cells that need it. During exercise, your brain signals your body to produce a hormone called epinephrine. Epinephrine is also known as adrenaline. This hormone signals the heart to pump faster. This moves more blood—and oxygen—to muscles that need it to keep your body moving.

The network of hundreds of muscles in the human body allow us to freely perform such a dynamic exercise as running.

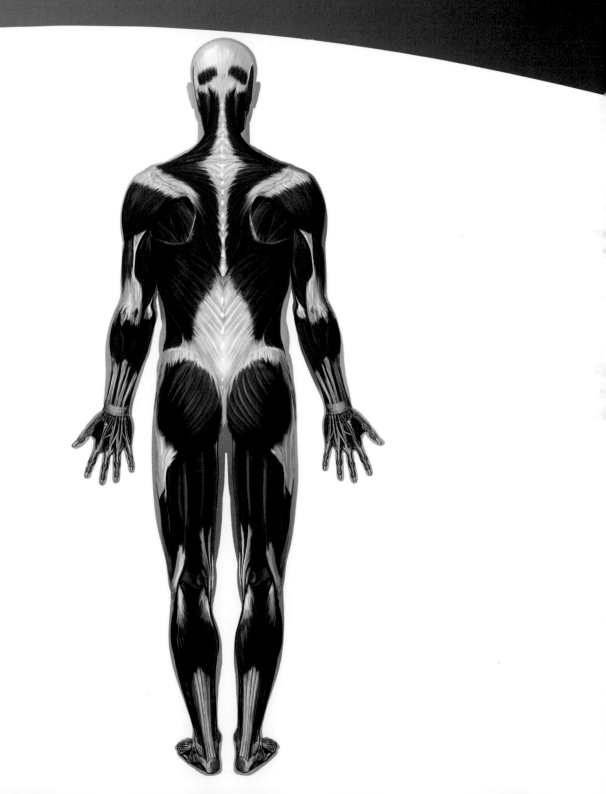

Your increased heart rate gets more oxygen-filled blood to your body. But your body is working hard during exercise and is using that oxygen faster than normal. This may cause carbon dioxide to build up in your blood. When there is too much carbon dioxide in your blood, you feel out of breath. Your brain detects the excess carbon dioxide and sends a signal to your diaphragm and other muscles around your lungs. The diaphragm speeds up your breathing rate and allows you to take in more oxygen.

The musculoskeletal system is the third important system when you exercise. Your bones and muscles support your body and allow you to move. Exercise helps make the bones and muscles of the musculoskeletal system strong and flexible. It also strengthens muscles like the diaphragm. Because your heart is a muscle, it needs regular exercise just as your leg or arm muscles do. One goal of exercise is to get your heart to beat faster, although not too fast. The following chapters will help you learn about the goals and benefits of exercise and running.

Getting the Most Out of Running

There are several things to consider before beginning running for exercise. First of all, it's a good idea to visit a family doctor and have a physical exam. A doctor can make sure you are healthy enough to begin a new exercise program. If you have any medical conditions, your doctor may monitor your exercise. This is especially important if you have any heart or breathing problems.

You may also want to talk to your physical education teacher at school. Or you could talk to a fitness professional at a gym. He or she may be able to help you create a good plan for how much and how often you should run.

How Much Should You Run?

One of the first things to think about is how much you should run. It is a very good idea to set time goals, not distance goals. Plan to run for twenty minutes, for example, instead of 2 miles (3.2 kilometers). Increase time slowly. You need to add only a minute or two each time you run. Adding less than a minute each time is fine, too, as long as you continue to increase your time. Exactly how much time you add is not important.

When you first begin running, you may find it easier to combine walking and running. For example, you could run for one minute and walk for one

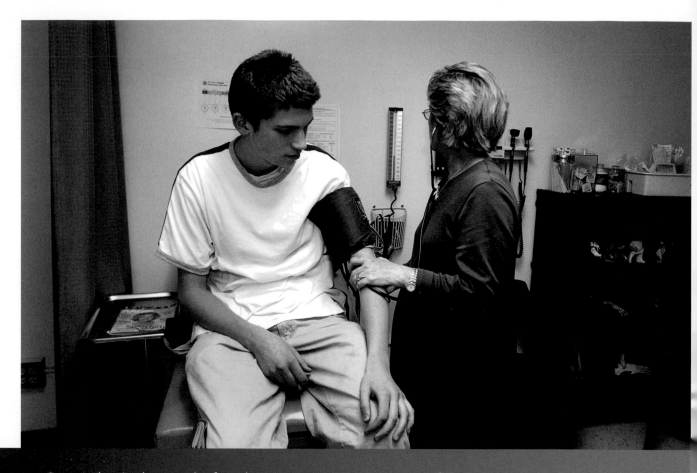

Get a physical exam before beginning any new type of exercise. If you have a medical condition, such as asthma or diabetes, your doctor can help you plan a safe routine.

minute. Build up slowly so you run more and walk less. Eventually, you will be able to run for your whole session.

Instead of running fast, run at a comfortable pace. You should be able to run without breathing too hard or struggling to breathe. A good way to test this is to see whether or not you can talk while you are running. If you can't talk easily, you're probably running too fast.

As you just learned, how far you run is less important than how long you run. However, if you are under fourteen years old, you should run less than 3 miles

Running is a great way to have fun, get fit, feel great, and even improve your mood.

(about 5 km) at a time. This is because your bones are still growing. The areas where your bones are growing are softer than adult bones. This makes children more likely to be injured by running too far. This is one of the reasons that most marathons don't let children under eighteen enter.

How Often Should You Run?

There is no one perfect plan that fits every person. So keep in mind that you may be able to run more—or less—often than other runners you know. At least to start, you should aim to run three times a week. It is OK if you need to combine running with walking to meet that goal. Once you feel comfortable running three times a week, consider increasing the number of days you run. But you should allow your body enough time to rest between runs. That will help you avoid injuries.

Water's Essential Role

More than 60 percent of your body is water. It is essential for many functions. Water helps get rid of waste and move food through the body. It helps your body maintain steady temperature and blood pressure. Water also helps keep your joints in good working order.

Water is all you really need while running, but sports drinks can be good, too. Sports drinks contain glucose (sugar) and sodium (salt), as well as water. Glucose provides your body with energy. Sodium helps keep enough water in your blood. Some sports drinks also contain extra vitamins or herbs. You don't really have to have these added ingredients. Water, glucose, and sodium are all you need.

Providing Your Body with the Right Fuel

One important thing you can do for your body is to give it healthy food. Think of it like putting gas in a car. A car can't run without gas, and your body can't run

Bread is a good source of carbohydrates, which help fuel your body. Whole-grain breads are an especially healthy option.

without food. Make sure you eat before a run so your body has the fuel it needs. However, don't eat so much or so soon before a run that you feel full or uncomfortable while running.

Foods that are high in carbohydrates give your body lots of energy. Bread, pasta, potatoes, and rice are examples of foods high in carbohydrates. Foods high in carbohydrates are also easy for your body to digest. That is another reason why they are good to eat before running. But you should not eat just before a run. If possible, eat about three hours before you start running.

No matter what time of day you run, eating a good breakfast is very important. It gives your body the nutrients it needs after a night without eating. Also, if you have eaten a good breakfast, you will be less hungry throughout the day. This means you'll be less likely to make bad food choices.

Guidelines for Healthy Eating

It is best to eat fresh foods instead of processed or packaged foods. For example, a baked potato is much better than potato chips. Fresh fruit is better than fruit juice (which usually has extra sugar and other additives). It is especially important to eat plenty of fresh fruits and vegetables.

You should also aim to eat a balanced diet. This means eating from all of the major food groups. The food groups are grains, vegetables, fruits, milk, meat and beans, and oils. The U.S. Department of Agriculture's food pyramid is a good resource for information on the food groups. Aiming for a good variety of food is also important. That way, you can be sure you are getting all the vitamins and nutrients you need.

You also need to be sure you are eating the right amount of calories per day. In general nutrition terms, calories are a measure of how much energy a type of food will help your body produce. The more calories you eat, the more energy your body will be able to call on. However, if you eat more calories than your body uses up, your body will begin to store that extra energy as fat. Too many calories and you will gain weight. Too few calories and you will lose weight. Therefore, you need to try to eat just enough calories for your body to use in a day.

Boys eleven to fourteen years old need about 2,220 calories per day. Boys fifteen to eighteen years old need about 2,755. Girls eleven to fourteen years old need about 1,845 calories per day. Girls fifteen to eighteen years old need about 2,110 calories

Drinking water before, during, and after a run is important. Proper hydration allows your body to function at peak performance.

per day. However, if you get lots of exercise, you will probably need more calories than those given in general guidelines.

You may have heard the saying "everything in moderation." This is true for food choices. It's OK to have junk food once in a while. But you should eat it only once in a while and in small quantities.

Staying Hydrated

Drinking plenty of water while running is very important. You should drink while running and after running. This is especially important on hot days. When it is hot out, your body loses lots of water by sweating. You need to replace those lost fluids.

The Importance of Running Shoes

You don't need much special equipment for running. One thing you definitely need, however, is a good pair of running shoes. Good running shoes absorb the shock of your feet hitting the ground. This protects your feet and legs from injury. It is very important that your running shoes fit well. You want a snug fit. With a good size, your feet won't move around much in your shoes. This will help prevent blisters.

To get a good running shoe, go to a sports equipment or specialty running store. These types of stores have a wide selection so you can find the perfect shoe. They also have salespeople who know a lot about shoes and can help you get a good fit. Ask a salesperson to measure both of your feet. Most people's feet are not exactly the same size. Your shoes should fit your bigger foot. Make sure to try on both shoes to see if they both feel comfortable. Take a pair of running socks to the store with you and try on your shoes wearing your running socks. Walk (or run) around the store to test the fit and comfort. It's also a good idea to go shoe shopping near the end of the day. Throughout the day, your feet usually swell. You'll want to fit your shoes when your feet are at their largest.

Where Should You Run?

One of the good things about running is that you can do it nearly anywhere. However, some surfaces are better for running than others. It's best to run on dirt surfaces. These are softer and easier on your feet and legs. Indoor or outdoor tracks are

Running on dirt surfaces is easy on your feet and legs. Local parks often have dirt paths especially for runners.

specially made for running, so they are a good option as well. Running on a treadmill can be a good choice, particularly during the winter.

Grass surfaces are soft, so they are another alternative. But if you run on grass, you'll need to watch out for holes or bumps that might be hidden by the grass.

Running on roads is fine if they are made of asphalt. However, you'll need to be careful of potholes and cars. You should also avoid the side of the road if it slopes downward. Running on uneven surfaces can cause leg problems.

It is not a good idea to run on concrete or other very hard surfaces. This is because they can cause leg problems. Most sidewalks are made of concrete, so try to limit how much time you use them.

Stretching is recommended before and after you run. Ask your doctor or a fitness professional to help you plan a good stretching routine.

When Should You Run?

You can run at nearly any time of day. There are a few safety concerns to keep in mind, though. If you run very early in the morning or late in the evening, be sure to wear reflective clothing. You may also want to run with a friend or family member for extra safety. Running with a partner is a good idea at any time of day.

You should also keep the temperature in mind when determining when to run. During the heat of summer, you may want to run early in the day or in the early evening. Running in the heat of the day can be dangerous in very humid weather. During the winter, you may want to run in the mid- to late afternoon, when temperatures are highest. Also, during the winter, use common sense about surface conditions. Avoid icy roads, tracks, and sidewalks. Run indoors instead if you can.

Health Benefits

Regular exercise can strengthen many parts of your body. Exercise can help build three things: endurance, power, and strength.

Endurance is also sometimes called stamina. You build endurance when your muscles are working at their full capacity over a period of time. Endurance increases your ability to perform an exercise longer.

Building endurance is especially important for runners. Any exercise that builds endurance also strengthens your heart. Remember, your heart is a muscle. A stronger heart is better able to pump blood throughout your body effectively. This can help keep your arteries clear.

Lowering Your Risk of Illness

Many studies have shown that regular exercise (including running) lowers your risk of getting some diseases, such as cancer and heart disease. It also lowers your risk of developing health problems, such as high blood pressure, type 2 diabetes, and osteoporosis.

People who exercise regularly also tend to live longer than people who don't. Any exercise is better than none, but more exercise has better results. If you work out harder, longer, and more frequently, you will get more benefits to your health.

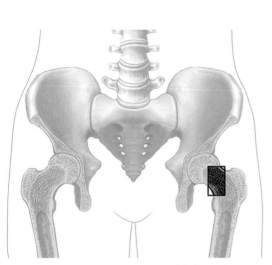

Bone section
through hip

Solid
bone matrix

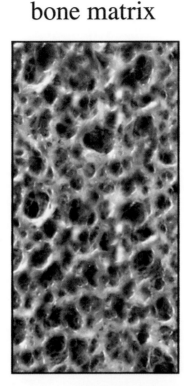

Weakened
bone matrix

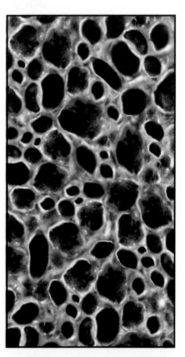

Running regularly can help prevent osteoporosis, a disease that weakens your bones. The illustration on the far right shows a bone with osteoporosis.

Maintaining or Losing Weight

Running is a great way to lose weight if you are overweight. If you are already at a healthy weight, running can help you stay that way.

Running is an excellent way to use—or burn—calories. Exactly how many you burn depends on how long and/or hard you run. The exact amount also depends on how much you weigh. In general, you can burn anywhere from 500 to 900 calories

Exercise can help you focus better on schoolwork. Some studies have shown that students who exercise regularly can improve their test scores.

per hour of running. (These numbers are for a person who weighs 100 pounds [45 kilograms].) This is more than other active sports. For example, soccer burns about 400 calories per hour. Biking burns about 250 calories per hour.

Improving Your Mind and Your Mood

People who exercise regularly usually feel more alert after working out. Scientists are studying the link between exercise and the brain. A recent study by the California Department of Education shows that children who are physically fit score higher on standard achievement tests than students who are not as physically fit.

Exercise also causes your body to produce hormones called endorphins. These hormones can lower your level of stress. Endorphins also improve your mood.

Fighting Illness

A healthy body is much better equipped to fight off illness. People who are in good physical condition and have lower levels of stress are less likely to get a cold or the flu, for example.

However, some experts believe that too much exercise can have the opposite effect. If you don't allow enough time for your body to rest between exercise sessions, it may affect your immune system. Working out too hard can also have a negative effect on your immune system. This makes you less likely to be able to fight off colds or other illnesses spread by germs.

Avoiding Injury

There are several things you can do to avoid injury. One of the best things you can do is to stretch before you begin running. Stretching helps you avoid injuring yourself because it increases your flexibility. The more flexible you are, the better able your body will be to protect against damage to muscles and joints. Stretching also gets your blood flowing to every part of your body. When stretching, go slow and be gentle. Don't stretch too far or make sudden movements. Don't hold your breath while stretching. Instead, make sure to breathe in and out slowly and steadily. Try to hold each stretch for thirty seconds to one minute. Don't stretch until it hurts. If you feel pain, you are probably stretching your muscles too hard.

You should also warm up before a run and cool down slowly afterward. Walking is an excellent warm-up and cool-down activity. Warming up will give your body a chance to get loose beforehand. It's also another good way to get blood flowing to all parts of your body. A slow-down walk after a run will have the opposite effect.

A few additional tactics will help you avoid injury. As mentioned earlier, you should not run every single day. Your body needs time to recover between runs. This is especially true for your legs.

It's also important to keep your muscles loose. While running, keep your hands, face, and shoulders relaxed. Run as lightly as possible, rather than pounding the pavement.

Use common sense in deciding what's best for you and your running routine. Remember to consult your family doctor or a coach or teacher with specific questions. They can help you choose safe, healthy options.

Potential Drawbacks

Although running has many potential benefits to your health, it can have some negative effects. Several types of injuries are more common for runners—especially injuries to the legs and feet and joints. Running in extreme cold or heat can cause problems for runners. Not drinking enough water (and sometimes drinking too much) can cause problems, too. And in some cases, people can become addicted to running (or exercise in general).

Runner's Injuries

Injuries happen most often in the parts of the body that get the most use during running: feet, legs, knees, and hips. There are ways to avoid injury in the first place. A good stretching routine and warming up and cooling down can help. Wearing shoes that fit well and giving your body a chance to rest between runs are other good ways to avoid injury.

Common feet problems are blisters and plantar fasciitis, which causes pain in your heel. Other feet problems involve the ankle. Ankle sprains and tendonitis often occur in runners. Leg problems for runners include shin splints and pulled muscles. Long-distance runners also commonly get stress fractures. These are bone breaks caused by repetitive motion.

Knees and hips are other body areas that can be injured from

Stretching before a run can help prevent foot, ankle, knee, and leg injuries, such as sprains and pulled muscles.

running. Both are joints, and they absorb a lot of the stress of repetitive motion. Both knees and hips can get stress fractures. The muscles, tendons, and ligaments surrounding both joints can also be injured.

Heat and Cold

You need to take a little more care when you run in extremely hot or extremely cold weather. Your body can usually regulate its temperature well to adapt to weather conditions. However, extreme heat and cold can cause problems. In the summer, you must watch out for heat exhaustion and heat stroke. In hot weather, your body sweats to keep its temperature down. When you are running in hot weather, your body may not be able to keep up with the cooling process. This can lead to muscle cramps (called heat cramps) and heat exhaustion. If you have heat exhaustion, you may feel faint, have a headache and muscle aches, and may sweat more than normal. You may also feel nauseous. To treat heat exhaustion, drink plenty of water or sports drinks. Try to get somewhere cool as soon as possible.

If you don't treat heat exhaustion, you may develop heat stroke. Heat stroke is a much more serious condition. Heat stroke occurs when your body can no longer regulate body temperature and internal temperature rises too high. If you have heat stroke, you will stop sweating and have a high temperature, and you may

Track, Cross Country, and Marathons

If you want to test your running skills against other runners, there are three ways to compete. In track events, the focus is on speed. You compete against other runners in specific distances. Cross-country competitions feature races over distances, but not on tracks or roads. Some cross-country races may even go through mud or water. Marathons are distance events. Most marathons are 26.2 miles (42.2 km) long.

hyperventilate. Heat stroke can lead to death, so it is important to treat it as soon as possible. Call a doctor or 911 if you think you have heat stroke.

During the winter, you need to be aware of the potential of developing hypothermia. You can get hypothermia if your body can't produce enough heat to make up for what is lost. If you have hypothermia, your body slows down and you can't think clearly. You may also shiver uncontrollably.

You can avoid all of these conditions by using common sense when exercising in extreme weather. During the summer, try to exercise in the coolest parts of the day, such as early morning. Wear cool, loose, light-colored clothing. Drink plenty of water or sports drinks. Take breaks in the shade or other cool areas.

This runner was treated for heat exhaustion after a track event. Getting treatment for heat exhaustion can prevent you from developing heat stroke, a more serious condition.

During the winter, try to exercise in the warmest part of the day (usually mid-day). Wear several layers of clothes. The layer closest to your body should be a material that absorbs sweat to keep your body dry. Cotton and specially made sports gear will do this. Make your top layer waterproof. Wear a hat and gloves, and wear a scarf or face mask over your mouth. This will warm up the air that is going into your lungs.

Water: Too Little or Too Much

When you run, your body sweats (even in cold weather). This helps keep your body from overheating. The drawback is that you lose a lot of the water that your body needs. If you don't replace the water by drinking, you can become dehydrated. With less water in your bloodstream, your heart has to work harder to pump. Less water in your body can give you muscle cramps. If you are dehydrated, you will probably also feel tired.

You lose more water by sweating on hot days, but you can become dehydrated in cool weather, too. No matter what the weather, make sure you drink before and after a run. If you're going for a long run, or if the weather is very hot, try to drink during your run, too.

It is possible to drink too much water. Drinking too much can lead to a condition called hyponatremia. If you drink too much, you lower the amount of sodium (salt) in your bloodstream. If the amount of salt in your blood gets too low, it can cause a seizure. Hyponatremia can also cause death in some cases. Hyponatremia happens to women more often than men. This is probably because women are generally smaller than men. They also sweat less than men. If women drink too much, they don't have as much of a chance to sweat out the excess water.

You are not likely to get hyponatremia during a short run or regular workout. It is more likely to occur during a long run, such as a marathon. Do be careful not to drink too much water. If you have to drink a lot, you may want to have a sports drink instead of water. Sports drinks contain added sodium (salt). This can keep the amount of salt in your bloodstream in good balance.

Addiction

It is possible to become addicted to exercise, and therefore to running. When you exercise, your body produces hormones called endorphins. These hormones produce

Though running is healthy, some people overexert themselves and even grow addicted to the "runner's high," or the euphoric feeling some people get from the exercise.

feelings in your body similar to that of a high. This is what you might sometimes hear called a "runner's high."

Just as people can become addicted to feelings produced by drugs, they can become addicted to feelings produced by endorphins. However, to get these same effects every time you exercise, eventually you need larger and larger doses of endorphins. To produce the good feelings requires more frequent and longer runs. As you have already read, if you don't allow your body to rest enough between runs, you are more likely to be injured.

People can become addicted to other effects from exercise. For example, people might lose a lot of weight due to running or other exercise. Some of these people may want to keep losing more and more weight. This can lead to overexercise. Too much weight loss might also lead to anorexia nervosa or other problems caused by low body weight.

New Developments in Running

The U.S. government has developed new guidelines for how much and what kinds of exercise you should get. The new guidelines recommend that children and teenagers should do an hour or more of physical activity each day. Most of that hour should be moderate or vigorous aerobic activity. Examples of moderate aerobic activity include hiking, skateboarding, fast walking, mowing the lawn or raking leaves, and playing catch. Soccer, swimming, cross-country skiing, basketball, bike riding, tennis, and running are several examples of vigorous aerobic activity. The guidelines recommend that at least three days a week your hour of activity should include a vigorous activity.

At least three days a week, your physical activity should also include a muscle-strengthening activity. These kinds of activities force your muscles to do more work than they would during a normal, daily activity. Examples of muscle-strengthening activities are doing sit-ups, push-ups, or pull-ups; using a climbing wall; or using weights.

The third type of recommended physical activities are those that strengthen your bones. Bone-strengthening activities put pressure on your bones that causes them to grow and get stronger. At least three days a week, you should include bone-strengthening activities in your hour of daily activity. Examples of these types of activities are jumping rope, running, gymnastics, basketball, and volleyball.

Taking Your Pulse

One way to measure your heart rate during exercise is by taking your pulse. You can feel your pulse in several places, but it is usually easiest to find on your wrist. Put a finger on your wrist, near your thumb, and feel around for your heartbeat. Using a clock or watch with a second hand, count the number of heartbeats in one minute. Take your pulse before and during exercise to see the difference in your heart rate.

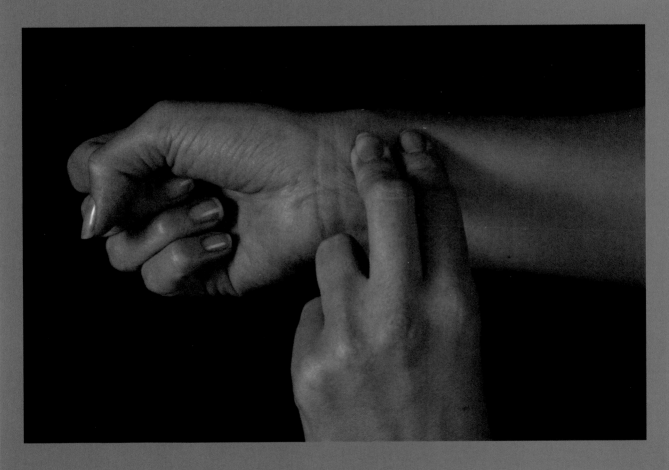

Your pulse rate before exercising is your resting rate. When you are exercising, it is called your active rate. The length of time it takes to go from active back to resting is known as recovery time.

You can see that there is some overlap in the three types of activities. For example, running is both an aerobic activity and a bone-strengthening activity. To fully meet the requirements, you could combine running with muscle-strengthening activities several days a week. You should also vary your routine by doing other kinds of aerobic and bone-strengthening activities. This will work different muscles and give your body a chance to rest.

Two types of exercise help you build endurance: aerobic and anaerobic. Aerobic exercise is exercise at a steady pace that uses the skeletal muscles. When you do aerobic exercise, your body needs more oxygen. This helps strengthen your heart and increase your lung capacity. Running is a good example of an aerobic exercise.

On days when you don't run, try participating in a vigorous aerobic activity, such as basketball, skating, tennis, or soccer.

Swimming and biking are two other examples. Anaerobic exercise is a short, intense amount of exercise. It makes your muscles work hard, and it uses up the oxygen in your body. Sprinting is a good example of an anaerobic exercise.

Power is the ability of your muscles to get to top strength quickly. This is especially important for gymnasts, for example. It can also come in handy for runners who need to start quickly in a race. Strength is the ability of muscles to apply force. A weigh lifter would want to build strength. Runners might also want to build strength in their legs.

Any exercise that makes you breathe faster also strengthens the muscles around your lungs. This is particularly true for your diaphragm, a strong muscle located below

Because shoes are important to the health of your legs and feet, replace them when the soles are worn out. Most runners replace their shoes every six months to a year.

your lungs. The stronger your diaphragm and other muscles surrounding the lungs are, the greater the amount of air your lungs can hold. This is called your lung capacity. A greater lung capacity allows you to take in and get rid of more air per breath.

The Latest Shoe Developments

Running shoe companies are always working on new features for their shoes. Some of the latest shoes feature new ways to lace up the shoe for a tighter fit. Other new shoes are very, very light. Another new type of shoe contains a GPS (global positioning system) transmitter. One new shoe is even biodegradable. It has a special type of foam in the heel that will break down when the shoe is in a landfill. The most important thing to keep in mind about shoes is comfort and fit. It's not necessary to buy a shoe that is the most trendy or the most expensive.

Now that you know more about exercise and running, it's time to get started. Get a physical exam from your doctor and a good pair of shoes. Then start running! Your body will be glad you did.

GLOSSARY

additive A substance added to food.

anorexia nervosa An eating disorder in which people fear gaining weight.

asphalt A substance used for paving roads.

carbohydrates Sugars and starches present in food.

carbon dioxide A gas produced by your body.

coordination The act of body parts working together smoothly and gracefully.

esophagus A muscular tube that joins the mouth and the stomach.

gland An organ that removes substances from the blood or stores substances to be released later.

hormone A substance made by your body that circulates in the blood and has specific effects on the body.

hyperventilate To breathe rapidly and deeply.

moderation Of even intensity.

nauseous Feeling sick or needing to vomit.

nutrients Substances your body needs.

nutrition Giving your body the substances it needs.

osteoporosis A condition in which your bones become less dense.

oxygen A gas present in air and water.

physiology The study of the functions and activities of the human body.

posture The position of the body.

seizure A sudden attack, sometimes including convulsions.

type 2 diabetes A health disorder that usually occurs in overweight people.

FOR MORE INFORMATION

Kids Running America
16261 Hollyridge Drive
Parker, CO 80134
(720) 260-2745
Web site: http://www.kidsrunningamerica.org
This organization promotes healthy and safe running. It sponsors a marathon
program for kids. You can run a portion of a marathon over a series of days
or weeks, and then the remainder at a local marathon.

Office of Disease Prevention and Health Promotion (ODPHP)
National Health Information Center
P.O. Box 1133
Washington, DC 20013-1133
(800) 336-4797
Web site: http://odphp.osophs.dhhs.gov
The ODPHP has developed guidelines for physical activity for Americans of all ages.

President's Council on Physical Fitness and Sports (PCPFS)
Department W
200 Independence Avenue SW
Room 738-H
Washington, DC 20201-0004
(202) 690-9000
Web site: http://www.fitness.gov
The PCPFS is a group of doctors, sports and fitness experts, and professional athletes
who advise the president on fitness and health.

Sport Canada
Canadian Heritage
15 Eddy Street, 16th Floor
Gatineau, QC K1A 0M5

Canada
(866) 811-0055
Web site: http://www.pch.gc.ca/pgm/sc/index-eng.cfm
Sport Canada aims to increase participation in sports in Canada.

Web Sites

Due to the changing nature of Internet links, Rosen Publishing has developed an online list of Web sites related to the subject of this book. This site is updated regularly. Please use this link to access the list:

http://www.rosenlinks.com/hwe/run

FOR FURTHER READING

Barrios, Dagny Scott. *Complete Book of Women's Running: The Best Advice to Get Started, Stay Motivated, Lose Weight, Run Injury-Free, Be Safe, and Train for Any Distance*. New York, NY: Rodale, 2007.

Branner, Toni. *The Care and Feeding of an Athlete: What You Need to Know to Rise to the Top of Your Game*. Waxhaw, NC: Blue Water Press, 2007.

Daniels, Jack. *Daniels' Running Formula*. Champaign, IL: Human Kinetics, 2005.

Evans, Lynette. *Move Your Bones*. New York, NY: Children's Press, 2008.

Fitzgerald, Matt. *Performance Nutrition for Runners: How to Fuel Your Body for Stronger Workouts, Faster Recovery, and Your Best Race Times Ever*. New York, NY: Rodale, 2006.

Goodger, Beverley. *Exercise*. North Mankato, MN: Smart Apple Media, 2006.

MacNeill, Ian, and The Sport Medicine Council of British Columbia. *The Beginning Runner's Handbook: The Proven 13-Week Walk/Run Program*. Vancouver, BC: Greystone Books, 2005.

Manocchia, Pat. *Anatomy of Exercise*. Buffalo, NY: Firefly Books, 2008.

Middleton, Haydn. *A World-Class Marathon Runner: The Making of a Champion*. Chicago, IL: Heinemann, 2004.

Shivers, Joseph, and Paul Shivers. *Harriers: The Making of a Championship Cross Country Team*. Uniontown, OH: Fresh Writers Books, 2006.

Snyder, Zilpha Keatley. *Cat Running*. New York, NY: Bantam Doubleday Dell, 1994.

Swan, Bill. *Mud Run*. Toronto, ON: James Lorimer & Company, Ltd., 2003.

Whiting, Jim. *Ultra Running with Scott Jurek*. Hockessin, DE: Mitchell Lane Publishers, 2007.

BIBLIOGRAPHY

American Council on Exercise. "Children and Running." Retrieved September 10, 2008 (http://www.acefitness.org/fitfacts/fitfacts_display.aspx?itemid=205).

Burfoot, Amby. *Complete Book of Running*. New York, NY: Rodale, Inc., 2005.

Manocchia, Pat. *Anatomy of Exercise*. Buffalo, NY: Firefly Books, 2008.

McArdle, William D., Frank I. Katch, and Victor L. Katch. *Exercise Physiology: Energy, Nutrition, and Human Performance*. 5th ed. Philadelphia, PA: Lippincott Williams & Wilkins, 2001.

Ratey, John J., MD, with Eric Hagerman. *Spark: The Revolutionary New Science of Exercise and the Brain*. New York, NY: Little, Brown and Company, 2008.

U.S. Department of Health and Human Services. "2008 Physical Activity Guidelines for Americans." 2008. Retrieved October 9, 2008 (http://www.health.gov/paguidelines).

Wuest, Deborah A., and Charles A. Bucher. *Foundations of Physical Education, Exercise Science, and Sport*. 15th ed. Boston, MA: McGraw Hill, 2006.

INDEX

About the Author

Simone Payment has a degree in psychology from Cornell University and a master's degree in elementary education from Wheelock College. She is the author of twenty-one books for young adults. Her book *Inside Special Operations: Navy SEALs*, also from Rosen Publishing, won a 2004 Quick Picks for Reluctant Young Readers Award from the American Library Association and is on the Nonfiction Honor List of Voice of Youth Advocates.

Photo Credits

Cover and interior (silhouetted figures, stripe graphics) © www.istockphoto.com/ Brandon Laufenberg; cover and interior (silhouetted figures) © www.istockphoto. com/Nicholas Monu; cover, p. 1 (circulatory system figure) © www.istockphoto.com/ Mads Abildgaard; p. 5 © Celin Serbo/Aurora Photos/Corbis; pp. 7, 11, 25 Nucleus Medical Art/Visuals Unlimited, Inc.; p. 8 LifeART image © 2010 Lippincott Williams & Wilkins. All rights reserved; p. 14 © Ellen B. Senisi/The Image Works; p. 15 © www.istockphoto.com/Michael Krinke; pp. 17, 19, 21, 39 Shutterstock.com; p. 22 © Anthony West/Corbis; p. 26 © Will & Deni McIntyre/Corbis; p. 30 (top) © www.istockphoto.com/Jacom Stephens; p 30 (bottom) © www.istockphoto.com/ technotr; p. 32 © AP Images; p. 34 © David Reed/Impact/HIP/The Image Works; p. 37 © www.istockphoto.com/David Kneafsey; p. 38 © www.istockphoto.com/ Jim Kolaczko.

Designer: Nicole Russo; Editor: Nicholas Croce;
    Photo Researcher: Cindy Reiman